Best Halloween Drink Recipes

Spooktacularly Delicious Halloween Drinks

I0157475

Diana Loera

Note from the Author

Please note – the softcover version of this book is a generous 8 ½ x 11 in size.

I hate squinting at tiny recipe books and don't think that you should have to do so either.

I create all of my books, especially the recipe books, in the larger size format for your reading ease.

I have included some color photographs but my publisher informed me that the more color photos, the higher the book cost must be- so I have tried to be selective with the photos included. Thank you for understanding.

Sincerely,

Diana

Introduction

With a hint of fall in the air, I'm already planning my fall and winter holiday parties.

Halloween parties are always fun and they seem to be the official kick off for the holiday season.

From elegant to casual entertaining, your guests will be impressed when you serve any or a combination of these wonderful Halloween themed drinks.

Some of the recipes, especially the pumpkin themed ones, can also be served at Thanksgiving parties too.

Of course, please ensure your guests have a designated driver and that everyone drinks responsibly.

Table of Contents

Other Books by Diana Loera

12 Extra Special Summer Dessert Fondue Recipes http://tinyurl.com/q7gpgw8

14 Extra Special Winter Holidays Fondue Recipes http://tinyurl.com/lkebggx

Awesome Thanksgiving Leftovers Revive Guide http://tinyurl.com/prxjayg

Best 100 Calorie or Less Dessert Recipes http://tinyurl.com/pn5b46c

Best Bacon Infused Dessert Recipes: 20 Mouthwatering Delicious Desserts Infused with Bacon http://tinyurl.com/owxo3pl

Coca Cola Ham, Coca Cola Cake and Other Coca Cola Recipes http://tinyurl.com/pp2wvhz

Party Time Chicken Wing Recipes http://tinyurl.com/ohsc9x8

Summertime Sangria http://tinyurl.com/oxnlnhm

Best Bacon Infused Dessert Recipes http://tinyurl.com/q38aaox

Best Copycat Recipes on the Planet http://tinyurl.com/pcuj24q

Best Pumpkin Recipe http://tinyurl.com/oxdr8fq

Best West Virginia Recipes http://tinyurl.com/oqywpbq

Best Pumpkin Drink & Dessert Recipes http://tinyurl.com/nmwx3mb

Please visit www.LoeraPublishingLLC.com to see our complete selection of books. Topics include cooking, travel, recipes, how to, non- fiction and more.

Spiced Pumpkin Cider

Yields about 2 cups

Ingredients:

1 cup pumpkin puree (not pumpkin pie mix)
2 1/2 cups apple cider
1/3 cup spiced rum - optional
1-1/2 teaspoons pumpkin pie spice
Cinnamon stick

Directions:

In a large pot, mix together the pumpkin puree, apple cider, pumpkin pie spice and the cinnamon stick.

Bring mixture to a boil then reduce heat to low and simmer for at least 20 minutes.

If mixture is too thick, add additional cider or water to thin it out.

Strain the mixture through a mesh strainer to remove clumps and cinnamon stick.

Add rum and mix. Serve warm.

You can reduce the amount of rum if this is too strong or omit it completely and swap in more apple cider.

Garnish with a cinnamon stick for additional eye appeal.

Spiced Pumpkin Cider

Pumpkin Chai Latte

Yield: 2 cups

Ingredients:

¼ cup + 1 tablespoon (75 grams) pumpkin puree
2 tablespoons real maple syrup
1½ teaspoons vanilla
¼ teaspoon cinnamon
⅛ Teaspoon nutmeg
⅛ Teaspoon allspice
⅛ Teaspoon ginger

2 cups milk of your choosing

2 bags of black tea

Directions:

In a small saucepan, bring all the ingredients, except for the tea bags, to a boil over medium heat.

Remove the saucepan from the heat, add the tea bags, and let the tea bags steep for 2 minutes.

Remove tea bags and discard.

Stir mixture and then pour into regular or glass mugs.

Sprinkle with cinnamon before serving if desired.

Pumpkin Pie White Hot Chocolate

Makes 4 Servings

Ingredients:

3 cups milk
1 cup canned pumpkin puree
1/2 tsp. cinnamon
1/4 tsp. ginger
1/8 tsp. cloves
1/8 tsp. nutmeg
1 tsp. vanilla
4 oz. white chocolate, chopped
Pinch salt

Directions:

In a medium saucepan, stir together the milk, pumpkin and spices over medium heat just until the mixture begins to simmer.

Remove from heat and add in the chopped white chocolate and stir together until completely melted and fully blended.

If the mixture seems too thick or chunky, place in blender for 30 seconds to a minute.

Pour into mugs, top with whipped cream and sprinkle with cinnamon if desired.

Chocolate Pumpkin Cocktail

Ingredients per Serving:

2 oz. Rum
1 oz. Pumpkin puree (not pumpkin pie filling)
1/2 oz. Chocolate liqueur
1/2 oz. Pumpkin spice liqueur (optional)
1/2 oz. Simple syrup
2 oz. Pumpkin ice cream
Dash of cinnamon

Directions:

Combine all the ingredients in a cocktail shaker.

Fill with ice and shake well until the ice cream melts.

Pour into a chilled cocktail glass and garnish with a cinnamon stick.

Pumpkin Spice Whiskey Cocktail

Ingredients:

This is another per serving recipe

1 part Kahlua Pumpkin Spice
1 ½ parts Jameson Irish Whiskey

Directions:

Serve in an old-fashioned glass, over the rocks, with a larger sized ice cubes.

Kahlua Pumpkin Martini

Ingredients:

1 ½ parts Kahlua Pumpkin Spice
1 ½ parts ABSOLUT Vodka

Directions:

Combine ingredients in a cocktail shaker with ice, shake and strain into chilled martini glass.

Garnish with orange zest.

If you are serving at a Halloween party, definitely add extras to garnish and accent.

Kahlua Pumpkin Martini

Pumpkin Caipirinha

1/2 lime, cut into 4 pieces
1/2 oz. agave nectar
Crushed ice
1 1/2 oz. cachaça (can substitute white rum)
1 1/2 oz. pumpkin puree
1/2 oz. ginger liqueur (can substitute 1/2 oz. homemade ginger simple syrup or 1 tsp. freshly peeled and grated ginger)

For garnish:

Grated nutmeg
Lime wedge
Pumpkin sliver

If entertaining on Halloween, use accents such as Halloween cats, skulls etc.

Directions:

The base of this recipe uses cachaça — a popular distilled spirit from Brazil that is made from sugarcane. If you don't have cachaça, feel free to use rum instead. Both spirits are made from unrefined sugars, though cachaça tends to be a bit tarter and sharper.

In a cocktail shaker, combine lime and agave nectar (if using fresh ginger, add it at this time); muddle.

Add ice, cachaça, pumpkin puree, and ginger liqueur; shake well.

Garnish drink with grated nutmeg, pumpkin sliver, and lime wheel.

Makes one cocktail.

Pumpkin Caipirinha

Pumpkin Pie Milkshake Alcohol Infused

Serves about 2

Ingredients:

About 2-1/2 cups low-fat vanilla ice cream
1/3 cup Pinnacle Pumpkin Pie vodka
1/4 cup Coffee-Mate Pumpkin Spice creamer (Aldi's also carries their own store brand)
1-1/2 tablespoons brown sugar
1/2 cup pumpkin puree
1/2 teaspoon pumpkin pie spice
1 graham cracker, cut into bite-size pieces
Whipped cream

Directions:

Place all of the ingredients (minus the graham cracker) into a blender.

Blend on low until mixture is creamy.

If too thick, add additional creamer or vodka.

If not thick enough for your taste, add additional vanilla ice cream.

Garnish milkshakes with whipped cream, pumpkin pie spice and graham crackers.

Candy Corn Jello Shots

Prep time: 10 mins
Total time: 10 mins
Serves: 10-12 shot glasses (2 oz)

Ingredients:

1 small box lemon jello
1 small box orange jello
2 packets (3 tablespoons) Knox unflavored gelatin
2 cups boiling water
Cool Whip
Sprinkles for garnish, optional

Instructions:

In a small bowl, combine lemon jello and 1 packet of unflavored gelatin, stir

Add 1 cup boiling water and stir 2 minutes or until dissolved

Add jello to shot glasses, fill about ½ way

Place in fridge for 20 minutes

Repeat with 1 cup boiling water, orange jello and unflavored gelatin

Fill shot glasses and place in fridge for 20 minutes

Up to 1 hour before serving, add Cool Whip to the top and sprinkles if you like

Alcoholic version:

Add 1 cup boiling water to 1 box of Jello and stir to dissolve.

Add ¾ cup vodka and ¼ cup cold water, stir to combine

Add to shot glasses and chill

Note - this is for a single flavor

Notes:

You can easily double the recipe to serve more. Prep time does not include chilling time.

Candy Corn Jello Shot

Grave Digger Cocktail

Yield: 1 cocktail

Ingredients:

2 ounces Hard Cider
1 ounce Whiskey (Bourbon is often used)
Cold Ginger ale, to fill
Crushed ice

Instructions:

In a 12-16 ounce tumbler or high ball glass, combine the hard cider and whiskey. Fill the glass with crushed ice. Fill with ginger ale.

Vampire Cocktail

Ingredients:

2 cups raspberries
1/4 cup sugar
4 ounces vodka
2 ounces amaretto
2 ounces orange juice
6 ounces club soda
4 plastic syringes

Instructions:

Puree the raspberries in a blender or food processor. Press the puree through a fine mesh strainer to separate the pulp from the seeds. Discard the seeds.

Combine the puree with the sugar in a small saucepan over medium high heat. Stir frequently and cook until mixture darkens and thickens, about 10 minutes. Chill until ready to use.

Add vodka and amaretto to a shaker with ice and shake until very cold, about 20 seconds. Stir in orange juice and club soda. Pour into iced glasses.

Fill syringes with equal parts of the raspberry syrup and place in glasses before serving.

Witches Brew

Ingredients:

1 quart lime sherbet, softened just a bit
1 - 12 oz can. frozen limeade concentrate, thawed
1 liter Sprite or 7UP

Garnish with gummi eye balls or other Halloween themed gummi candies

Instructions:

Mix all ingredients in a punch bowl right before serving.

Witches Brew Punch

Witching Hour Black Sangria Recipe

Ingredients:

1 bottle Apothic Dark
2 cups blackberries, washed
4 black plums, washed and sliced
1/4 cup brandy
2 cups seedless black grapes, washed
1 cup sparkling water if you desire, but you don't have to if you want a strong wine taste.

Instructions:

Add everything into a non metallic pitcher and mix with a large spoon.

Let it sit in the refrigerator for 1 to 2 hours.

The longer it sits the deeper and darker the color becomes.

Witching Hour Black Sangria Recipe

Witching Hour Black Sangria

Creamy Butterbeer

Ingredients:

12 oz. (one bottle) ginger beer
36 oz. (three bottles) cream soda
3 T butterscotch ice cream topping

Instructions:

Thoroughly chill unopened ginger beer and cream soda in refrigerator until icy-cold. Refrigerate an empty glass pitcher also.
Once beverages are chilled, in a small mixing bowl or tall glass, stir 1-2 oz. of cream soda into butterscotch topping till thoroughly combined. Pour all remaining soda into chilled pitcher. Quickly add butterscotch mixture to pitcher. Stir till just combined; do not over-stir. Pour over ice and serve immediately. Serves 6.

Sparkle Version

For a frothy sparkle, dip the rim of each glass in corn syrup, pulling drips of syrup downward with a toothpick. Then dip each glass rim in a mixture of colored sugar. Before dipping, spread the corn syrup & sugar mixture each onto a separate, flat-bottomed plate.

Sugar Rim Version

For an old-world, textured effect, mix fine, yellow sugar with coarser, gold sugar. Colored sugars are available at many grocery stores and craft chains.

Halloween Fizz

Ingredients:

1 1/2 cups pineapple juice
1/4 teaspoon almond extract (or 1/2 cup rum)
1/4 teaspoon Imitation Coconut Extract
3 drops McCormick® Red Food coloring
2 drops McCormick® Yellow Food coloring
1 bottle Welches® sparkling white grape juice (or sparkling white wine)
Cranberries (optional)
2 tablespoons sugar
5 drops red food coloring
5 drops yellow food coloring

Instructions:

"Mix pineapple juice, almond extract, coconut extract and food coloring in a small picture or large measuring cup.

For each drink, pour 2 ounces pineapple juice mixture into beverage glass. Top with 4 ounces sparkling white grape juice.

How to Rim Glass with Orange-Tinted Sugar: Place 2 tablespoons sugar in small resealable plastic bag. Add 5 drops McCormick® Red Food Color and 5 drops Yellow Food Coloring. Seal bag. Knead sugar until the color is evenly distributed. Pour out onto shallow plate. Dip rim of beverage glass in water, then into Orange-tinted sugar to lightly coat.

To top it off, drop cranberries into the glass to float on top."

Bloody Shirley Temples

This non -alcoholic drink is fun for kids and for those who do not wish to have an alcoholic drink

Ingredients:

Sprite, chilled
Ice
Grenadine

Instructions:

Pour Sprite over ice, wait until it stops fizzing.

Squirt Grenadine in for a fun taste and look.

Hocus Pocus Halloween Cocktail

Serves: 2

Ingredients:

⅔ cup Paradise Blend Juice (Dole)
⅓ cup Coconut Rum
Club soda
Black sanding sugar (optional)
Honey (optional)
Ice (optional)

Instructions:

Prepare your glasses by applying a thin coating of honey to the rim of your glass. Roll glass onto a plate of black sanding sugar.

Mix juice and coconut rum together. Divide and pour into two prepared glasses. Add a couple of cubes of ice. Top the drink with club soda (2-4 ounces).

Creepy Eyeball Martini

Prep time: 15 mins
Cook time: 5 mins
Total time: 20 mins
Serves: 2

Ingredients:

4 ounces Vodka
3 ounces lychee syrup/juice (canned lychees, drained, reserve syrup/juice and lychees)
2 ounces Solerno Blood Orange Liqueur
1 ounce green tea simple syrup**

For the Simple Syrup:

6 oz water
6 oz cup sugar
1 Green tea bag (I used Double Green Matcha Tea - this gave the best green color)
Garnish:
Lychees
Blueberries
Skewers

Instructions:

For the Simple Syrup:

Bring water to a boil and pour into glass measuring cup. Let sit for one minute then add the green tea bag. Let steep 3 minutes. Remove the bag and add in the sugar, stir until dissolved then chill completely before using. This makes more than the drink calls for, store the remaining simply syrup in an airtight container in the refrigerator. Use it to sweeten other cocktails or even just a cup of green tea.

For the Cocktail:

Fill a cocktail shaker with ice, add in all the cocktail ingredients, shake well and divide between two martini glasses. Take a couple of the lychee fruits and put blueberries in them to make the "eyeballs" either sink a couple into the drinks or skewer and rest on top. Serve drinks chilled.

Headless Horseman Cocktail

Serves: 1

Ingredients:

1 ounce St. George Spirits NOLA coffee liqueur
¾ ounce mezcal
½ ounce Heering cherry liqueur
1 dash Fee Brother's Black Walnut Bitters
Homemade brandied cherry for garnish

Instructions:

Add coffee liqueur, mezcal, cherry liqueur and bitters to a cocktail shaker or mixing glass and fill with ice.

Stir and strain into a chilled cocktail glass.

Garnish with a brandied cherry.

Candy Corn Cocktail

Ingredients:

2 ounces candy corn vodka
3/4 ounce triple sec
1/2 ounce fresh squeezed lime

Instructions:

Add all ingredients into a cocktail shaker with ice.

Shake and strain into a chilled martini glass.

All Hallows Eve Cocktail

Ingredients:

2 ounces candy corn vodka
1 ounce creme de cocoa white
1/2 ounce Godiva white chocolate liqueur

Directions:

Add all ingredients into a cocktail shaker with ice.

Shake and strain into a chilled martini glass.

Blackbeard's Best

Ingredients:

1 oz spiced rum
1/2 oz Fernet Branca
1 1/2 oz crème de cacao
1/8 teaspoon squid ink (optional)
1/2 oz chocolate stout

Instructions:

Start by adding the spiced rum, Fernet, and crème de cacao to your shaker.

Next, add the squid ink. Careful, this stuff stains! You can find squid ink at your local fish market. You can also try a grocery store with a good fish counter, like Whole Foods. If you're squeamish, feel free to substitute black food coloring.

Give the ingredients a hard, dry shake (no ice). This will help thoroughly incorporate the ink.

Fill your shaker with ice and shake vigorously for a full 30 seconds so that your drink becomes cold and frothy. Double strain into a chilled cocktail glass and top with the chocolate stout.

Bat's Favorite Black Licorice Cocktail

Ingredients:

4 parts Pernod® licorice liqueur
3 parts black currant cordial
8 – 10 parts water
Black food coloring or icing coloring
1 cup sugar

Instructions:

Fill a pitcher with water, and add black food coloring in small increments until water reaches desired blackness.

Pour black water into ice tray and allow to freeze completely.

While ice is freezing, pour 1 cup sugar into a bowl. Add 1/4 tsp. black food coloring to the sugar and use a fork to mash until fully incorporated.

Dip the rims of your glasses into water, and then into the black sugar. Don't put too much water on the rims, as it'll cause the sugar to drip.

Add 1 or 2 cubes of black ice to each glass.

In a separate pitcher combine the Pernod, black currant cordial and water, and pour over ice cubes.

Garnish with Halloween bats or other Halloween themed garnish

Thank you

Thank you for taking a look at my Halloween drink recipes. I hope that you've found at least one or two that you plan on trying.

You can jazz up a Halloween party with the simple addition of Halloween themed garnishes. I often buy packs of skeletons and other Halloween themed party favors at the local dollar store. Usually the packages have 4 to 8 items so you can decorate 4 to 8 drinks or scatter the favors across your table settings.

Please remind your guests to drink responsibly and make sure they have a designated driver.

www.ingramcontent.com/pod-product-compliance
Lightning Source LLC
Chambersburg PA
CBHW042103040426
42448CB00002B/127